Collins

KS1 E|||||||||||||||

Grammar, Punctuation and Spelling

Grammar, Punctuation and Spelling

SATs Question Book

Age 6 – 7

Key Stage 1

SATs Question Book

Shelley Welsh

Contents

How to Use This Book

- You will need a pen or a pencil and a rubber.

- You must not use a dictionary or an electronic spell checker to answer any of the questions.

- The questions in this book are divided into sections: grammar, punctuation and vocabulary.

- There are different types of question for you to answer:

  - Some questions are multiple choice and require a tick in the box next to the correct answer.

  - Some require a word or phrase to be circled or underlined.

  - Some have a line or box for the answer.

  - Some questions ask for missing punctuation to be added.

- Always read the instructions carefully so you know how to answer each question.

- All questions are worth 1 or 2 marks.

- There are three progress tests throughout the book so that you can practise the skills again. Record your results in the progress charts to identify what you are doing well in and what you can improve.

Acknowledgements

The author and publisher are grateful to the copyright holders for permission to use quoted materials and images.

Every effort has been made to trace copyright holders and obtain their permission for the use of copyright material. The author and publisher will gladly receive information enabling them to rectify any error or omission in subsequent editions. All facts are correct at time of going to press.

Published by Collins
An imprint of HarperCollinsPublishers

1 London Bridge Street
London SE1 9GF

© HarperCollinsPublishers Limited 2018

ISBN 9780008253134

First published 2018

10 9 8 7 6 5 4 3 2 1

British Library Cataloguing in Publication Data.

A CIP record of this book is available from the British Library.

Author: Shelley Welsh
Commissioning Editors: Michelle l'Anson and Fiona McGlade
Editor and Project Manager: Katie Galloway
Cover and Inside Concept Design: Paul Oates
Text Design and Layout: Aptara® Inc
Production: Lyndsey Rogers
Printed and bound in China by RR Donnelley APS

Word Classes 1

1 What type of word is underlined in the sentence below?

I threw the ball over the <u>prickly</u> hedge.

Tick **one.**

an adverb ☐

a noun ☐

a verb ☐

an adjective ☐

1 mark

2 Circle the **verb** in the sentence below.

Megan   finished   her   homework   early.

1 mark

3 What type of word is underlined in the sentence below?

The dogs barked <u>loudly</u> when they saw the postman.

Tick **one.**

an adverb ☐

an adjective ☐

a verb ☐

a noun ☐

1 mark

Word Classes 1

4 Circle the **two adjectives** in the sentence below.

We ate a tasty snack of delicious strawberries.

○ I mark

5 What type of word is <u>running</u> in the sentence below?

Oscar saw two men running down the road.

Tick **one.**

a noun ☐

a verb ☐

an adverb ☐

an adjective ☐

○ I mark

6 Add a **suffix** to the word <u>clear</u> in the sentence below to make an **adverb**.

Gran could see <u>clear</u> _____ with her new glasses.

○ I mark

Total marks .... /6   How am I doing?

Word Classes 2

1 What type of words are underlined in the sentence below?

Maire walked down the <u>road</u> and into the <u>park</u>.

Tick **one.**

adverbs ☐

nouns ☐

verbs ☐

adjectives ☐

1 mark

2 Tick to show whether the underlined word in each sentence is an **adverb** or a **verb**.

Sentence	Adverb	Verb
Mia <u>quickly</u> brushed her teeth and then got dressed.		
Faiz <u>held</u> his new baby brother carefully in his arms.		
Two hens <u>crossed</u> the road right in front of our car.		
The wind blew <u>wildly</u> all night long.		

1 mark

3 Add a **suffix** to make each word an **adverb**.

firm_____

complete_____

1 mark

Word Classes 2

4 What type of word is underlined in the sentence below?

Mum <u>sang</u> quietly to the crying baby.

Tick one.

a verb ☐

a noun ☐

an adjective ☐

an adverb ☐

 1 mark

5 Tick the **two** verbs in the sentence below.

We finished our lunch before we went outside.

  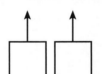

 1 mark

6 Tick the **three** nouns in the sentence below.

Joe is wearing a straw hat, shorts and a blue T-shirt.

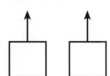

 1 mark

Total marks .... /6   How am I doing?

7

Word Classes 3

1 What type of words are underlined in the sentence below?

Our teacher told us to walk <u>quietly</u> but <u>quickly</u> to the school hall.

Tick **one.**

adverbs ☐

nouns ☐

verbs ☐

adjectives ☐

○ I mark

2 Circle the **adjective** in the sentence below.

A   beautiful   butterfly   landed   gracefully   on   the   flower. ○ I mark

3 What type of word is underlined in the sentence below?

My big sister <u>owns</u> a mobile phone.

Tick **one.**

an adverb ☐

a verb ☐

an adjective ☐

a noun ☐

○ I mark

Total marks .... /3   How am I doing?

Sentence Types 1

1 What type of sentence is below? The end punctuation is covered.

I play tennis on Saturdays

Tick **one.**

a command ☐

a question ☐

a statement ☐

an exclamation ☐

○ 1 mark

2 Draw a line to match each sentence to the type of sentence.

One has been done for you.

How many birthday cards did you get?	a statement
How exciting it was when you opened your presents!	a command
Everyone in the class was there.	a question
Write to your friends to say thank you for coming.	an exclamation

○ 1 mark

Sentence Types 1

3 Evie wants to invite Sam to her party.

Write a **question** she could ask him.

Remember to use correct punctuation.

_____

_____

_____

2 marks

4 Which punctuation mark completes all the sentences below?

It's cold today, isn't it

Can you tell me the time, please

Don't you feel tired after our busy day

Tick **one.**

a full stop ☐

an exclamation mark ☐

a question mark ☐

a comma ☐

1 mark

Total marks .... /5   How am I doing?

Sentence Types 2

1 Read the sentences below.

How lovely it was to see my grandparents at the weekend!

What an amazing surprise to see Uncle Jon!

How well he looked after his bad cold!

Tick the word that best describes these sentences.

Tick **one.**

questions ☐

exclamations ☐

statements ☐

commands ☐

1 mark

2 Read the sentences below.

Brush your teeth carefully.

Wash your face and hands.

Get into bed and go to sleep.

Tick the word that best describes these sentences.

Tick **one.**

questions ☐

exclamations ☐

statements ☐

commands ☐

1 mark

Sentence Types 2

3 Tick to show whether each sentence is a **statement**, **exclamation**, **command** or **question**.

Sentence	Statement	Exclamation	Command	Question
There are lots of flowers in the garden, aren't there?				
Mum loves to get flowers.				
Pick some flowers for Mum, please.				
How lovely those flowers are!				

◯
1 mark

4 Tick the sentence that is a **command**.

Tick **one.**

Finish your homework, please. ☐

Mum tidied my bedroom. ☐

What an amazing time we had! ☐

My teacher is going to Scotland in the summer. ☐

◯
1 mark

Total marks .... /4   How am I doing?

Sentence Types 3

1 The final punctuation mark is missing from each sentence below.

Tick the sentence that must have an **exclamation mark**.

Tick **one.**

Did you know that Zac was moving house ☐

How silly of me to forget your name ☐

It's your birthday tomorrow, isn't it ☐

Our dog sleeps on a mat in the kitchen ☐

1 mark

2 Ushma wants to know if her little brother, Ahmed, will play with her.

Write Ushma's **question** to Ahmed in the speech bubble.

Remember to use correct punctuation.

2 marks

Sentence Types 3

3 Which punctuation mark completes the sentence below?

What a fantastic day it has been

Tick **one.**

a question mark

a full stop

a comma

an exclamation mark

1 mark

4 Milo is going to tell Archie to give him his book back.

Write Milo's **command** to Archie in the speech bubble.

Remember to use correct punctuation.

2 marks

Total marks .... /6   How am I doing?

Forming Sentences

1 Tick the sentence that is written correctly.

Tick **one.**

Dad in the washing machine put his socks. ☐

Dad put his socks in the washing machine. ☐

Dad his socks put in the washing machine. ☐

Dad put the washing machine in his socks. ☐

◯ I mark

2 Write a sentence using the words in the boxes.

| hopped | The little bird | along the fence. |

Only use the words in the boxes.

Write your sentence on the lines below.

_____

_____

◯ I mark

3 Fabian's teacher asks him a question.

Complete the sentence below to show what his answer might be.

Remember to use correct punctuation.

Question: **Fabian, why is summer your favourite season?**

Answer: **Summer is my favourite season because** _____

_____

◯ I mark

Forming Sentences

4 Write a sentence using the words in the boxes.

| in my pencil case. | I put | and sharpener | my pencils, ruler |

Only use the words in the boxes.

Write your sentence on the lines below.

_____

_____ ◯
1 mark

5 Write a sentence to describe what you look like.

Remember to use correct punctuation.

_____

_____ ◯
1 mark

6 Tick the sentence that is written correctly.

Tick **one.**

Mum asked to tidy us up. ☐

Us asked Mum to tidy up. ☐

Mum to tidy up asked us. ☐

Mum asked us to tidy up. ☐ ◯
1 mark

Total marks .... /6   How am I doing?

Noun Phrases

1 Add an adjective to each **noun phrase** to expand it.

One has been done for you.

the ball   **the <u>bouncy</u> ball**

our puppy   **our _____ puppy**

the boy   **the _____ boy**

◯ I mark

2 Which sentence has a **noun phrase**?

Tick **one.**

We played tennis today. ☐

Dad likes painting. ☐

Mum bought a new red dress. ☐

We are learning about insects. ☐

◯ I mark

3 Underline the **noun phrase** in the sentence below.

The little kitten ate hungrily.

◯ I mark

4 Add a suitable **adjective** to the sentence below.

We watched the _____ lion climb up the mountainside.

◯ I mark

Noun Phrases

5 Write a **noun phrase** using the word <u>flower</u>.

_____

I mark

6 Tick to show the **two** sentences that have a **noun phrase**.

Sentences	Expanded noun phrase
We like healthy food.	
Our kind teacher never shouts.	
I like to listen to music.	
Mum enjoys gardening and golf.	

I mark

Total marks .... /6   How am I doing?

18

Joining Words

I Tick the correct word to complete the sentence below.

I wash my face _____ brush my teeth before I go to bed.

Tick **one.**

when ☐

and ☐

because ☐

if ☐

1 mark

2 Tick the correct word to complete the sentence below.

We could choose either ice cream _____ chocolate cake.

Tick **one.**

when ☐

if ☐

and ☐

or ☐

1 mark

3 Write one word on each line below to join the words and clauses to make a sentence.

Jamie _____ Alfie were allowed to play outside,

_____ Orla had to finish her work.

1 mark

19

Joining Words

4 Tick the correct word to complete the sentence below.

I asked Mum if I could watch TV, _____ she said no.

Tick **one.**

because ☐

if ☐

or ☐

but ☐

○ I mark

5 Which words complete the sentences below?

I have invited my cousins _____ my school friends to my party

on Friday, _____ my best friend can't make it. Mum says we

should change the date to either Saturday _____ Sunday.

Tick **one.**

if, or, but ☐

but, or, and ☐

and, but, or ☐

but, and, or ☐

○ I mark

Total marks .... /5	How am I doing?	

Using when, if, that and because

1 Tick the correct word to complete the sentence below.

Mum reads me a story _____ I am in bed.

Tick **one.**

but ☐

and ☐

that ☐

when ☐

◯ 1 mark

2 Tick the correct word to complete the sentence below.

Brogan put his coat on _____ it was raining.

Tick **one.**

but ☐

and ☐

because ☐

if ☐

◯ 1 mark

3 Write one word on each line below to join the clauses and make a sentence.

**I always clap _____ the team scores. _____
they are losing, I cheer them along.**

◯ 2 marks

Using when, if, that and because

4 Tick the correct word to complete the sentence below.

Joseph read the book _____ I bought him for his birthday.

Tick one.

if ☐

and ☐

because ☐

that ☐

1 mark

5 Which words complete the sentence below?

Dad was upset _____ his car wouldn't start _____ he left for work this morning.

Tick one.

that, because ☐

if, so ☐

because, when ☐

because, that ☐

1 mark

6 Write one word on each line below to complete the sentence.

I was given a special award _____ I got all my spellings right.

My teacher knew _____ I had worked really hard.

2 marks

Total marks .... /8   How am I doing? 😊 😐 😣

Past and Present Tense

1 Circle the correct verbs so that the sentence is in the **past tense**.

We | cycled | cycle | to school even though we | are | were | tired. ◯
                                                                      1 mark

2 Tick to show whether the sentence is in the **past tense** or the **present tense**.

Mum shops at the big shopping centre down the road.

Tick **one.**

present tense ☐

past tense ☐

◯
1 mark

3 Write the verb <u>like</u> in the **present tense** to complete the sentence below.

Jake _____ jigsaw puzzles.

◯
1 mark

23

Past and Present Tense

4 Tick to show whether each sentence is written in the **past tense** or the **present tense**.

Sentence	Past tense	Present tense
Charlotte tried hard to learn her spellings.		
My brother has blue eyes and blond hair.		
There are 30 children in my class.		

 1 mark

5 Write the verb <u>throw</u> in the **past tense** to complete the sentence below.

Sami _____ the ball to Mabel.

 1 mark

6 Circle the correct verbs so that the sentence is in the **present tense**.

Aziza | washes | washed | the dishes and Zainab | dried | dries | them.

 1 mark

Total marks .... /6   How am I doing?

Continuous Action

1 Circle the correct verbs so that the sentence is in the **past tense**.

The ducks | were quacking | | are quacking | as they

| swim | | swam | across the pond.

◯
1 mark

2 Write each verb in the **past tense** to show a **continuous action**.

One has been done for you.

Sentence	Verb
The dog <u>was barking</u> at the cat.	bark
The children _____ across the playground.	run
Madeleine _____ her hair.	brush

◯
2 marks

3 Write the verb <u>eat</u> in the **past tense** to show a **continuous action**.

Matthew _____ an apple when the phone rang.

◯
1 mark

4 Write the verb <u>work</u> in the **present tense** to show a **continuous action**.

The children _____ hard to learn their times tables.

◯
1 mark

Continuous Action

5 The verbs in boxes are in the **present tense**.

Write these verbs in the **past tense**.

One has been done for you.

Mum **<u>was saying</u>** that we eat too many sweets.

I told her we _____ to eat more fruit.

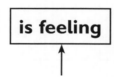

Mum said she _____ happier about
our next visit to the dentist.

2 marks

Total marks .... /7   How am I doing?

Using Tenses 1

1 Tick the sentence that is correct.

Tick **one.**

Our class went outside and plays games. ☐

Our class goes outside and played games. ☐

Our class went outside and played games. ☐

Our class go outside and plays games. ☐

○
1 mark

2 Write a **verb** in the **correct tense** to complete the sentence.

Last week, we went to the cinema and _____ Spiderman.

○
1 mark

3 Underline the **three verbs** that are in the **wrong tense**.

Yesterday, we go to the library to choose some books. I pick an adventure story and Maddie chose a book about tigers. When we get home, we started to read them before we had our dinner.

○
1 mark

Using Tenses 1

4 Rewrite the sentence in the **correct tense**.

Last week, we sing in assembly then walked quietly back to our classroom.

_____

_____ ◯
                                                 I mark

5 Tick the sentence that is correct.

Tick **one.**

When I go on holiday, I always took a book. ☐

When I went on holiday, I always take a book. ☐

When I go on holiday, I always take a book. ☐

When I went on holiday, I am always taking a book. ☐ ◯
                                                          I mark

6 Write **two** different **verbs** in the **present tense** to complete the sentences.

Usually, Dad _____ **us to school. On Fridays,**

we _____ **our bikes.** ◯
                                        I mark

Question	Requirement	Marks
	Pages 4–5 Word Classes 1	
1	an adjective ✓	1
2	**Megan (finished) her homework early.**	1
3	an adverb ✓	1
4	**We ate a (tasty) snack of (delicious) strawberries.**	1
5	a verb ✓	1
6	**Gran could see <u>clearly</u> with her new glasses.**	1
	Pages 6–7 Word Classes 2	
1	nouns ✓	1
2		1

Sentence	Adverb	Verb
Mia <u>quickly</u> brushed her teeth and then got dressed.	✓	
Faiz <u>held</u> his new baby brother carefully in his arms.		✓
Two hens <u>crossed</u> the road right in front of our car.		✓
The wind blew <u>wildly</u> all night long.	✓	

Question	Requirement	Marks
3	**firm<u>ly</u>** **complete<u>ly</u>**	1
4	a verb ✓	1
5	**We finished our lunch before we went outside.** ☑ ☐ ☐ ☑	1
6	**Joe is wearing a straw hat, shorts and a blue T-shirt.** ☐ ☑ ☑ ☑	1
	Pages 8 Word Classes 3	
1	adverbs ✓	1
2	**A (beautiful) butterfly landed gracefully on the flower.**	1
3	verb ✓	1
	Pages 9–10 Sentence Types 1	
1	a statement ✓	1
2	**How many birthday cards did you get?** – a question **How exciting it was when you opened your presents!** – an exclamation **Everyone in the class was there.** – a statement **Write to your friends to say thank you for coming.** – a command	1
3	Answers may vary. **Award 2 marks** for an appropriate question that starts with a capital letter and ends with a question mark, e.g. • *Will you come to my party, Sam?* • *Do you want to come to my party?* • *Sam, would you like to come to my party?* Also accept responses that do not use a capital letter for Sam or have incorrect internal punctuation.	Up to 2 marks

Answers

	Award 1 mark for an appropriate question that does not start with a capital letter and / or that does not end with a question mark, e.g. • *Would you like to come to my party* • *please will you come to my party Sam?*	
4	question mark ✓	1

Pages 11–12 Sentence Types 2		
1	exclamations ✓	1
2	commands ✓	1

3						1
	Sentence	**Statement**	**Exclamation**	**Command**	**Question**	
	There are lots of flowers in the garden, aren't there?				✓	
	Mum loves to get flowers.	✓				
	Pick some flowers for Mum, please.			✓		
	How lovely those flowers are!		✓			

4	**Finish your homework, please.** ✓	1

Pages 13–14 Sentence Types 3		
1	**How silly of me to forget your name** ✓	1
2	Answers will vary. **Award 2 marks** for an appropriate question that starts with a capital letter and ends with a question mark, e.g. • *Will you play with me Ahmed?* • *Do you want to play with me?* • *Ahmed, will you play?* Also accept responses that do not use a capital letter for Ahmed or have incorrect internal punctuation. **Award 1 mark** for an appropriate question that does not start with a capital letter and / or that does not end with a question mark, e.g. • *Would you play with me Ahmed* • *please will you play with me?*	Up to 2 marks
3	exclamation mark ✓	1
4	Answers will vary. **Award 2 marks** for an appropriate command that contains an imperative verb and ends with a full stop, e.g. • *Give me my book back, please.* • *Archie, give me my book.* Also accept responses that do not use a capital letter for Archie, have incorrect internal punctuation or end with an exclamation mark. **Award 1 mark** for an appropriate command that does not start with a capital letter and / or that does not end with a full stop, e.g. • *give me my book back, please.* • *Give me back my book*	Up to 2 marks

Pages 15–16 Forming Sentences		
1	**Dad put his socks in the washing machine.** ✓	1
2	*The little bird hopped along the fence.* Do not accept answers without capitalisation of 'The' or a full stop after 'fence'.	1
3	Answers will vary. Examples: **Summer is my favourite season because** *it is hot.* / **Summer is my favourite season because** *I like to play outside.* Do not accept answers without a final full stop.	1

4	*I put my pencils, ruler and sharpener in my pencil case.* Do not accept answers without capitalisation of 'I' or a full stop after 'pencil case'.	I
5	Answers will vary. The sentence must start with a capital letter and end with a full stop. Do not penalise spelling mistakes.	I
6	**Mum asked us to tidy up.** ✓	I

Pages 17–18 Noun Phrases		
I	Answers will vary. Examples: **our** *cute / sweet / playful* **puppy** **the** *naughty / kind / little* **boy** Do not penalise spelling mistakes if the intention is clear.	I
2	**Mum bought a new red dress.** ✓	I
3	<u>**The little kitten**</u> **ate hungrily.**	I
4	Answers will vary. Examples: **We watched the** *strong / fierce* **lion climb up the mountainside.** Do not penalise spelling mistakes if the intention is clear.	I
5	Answers will vary. Examples: *the beautiful / colourful / yellow flower* Also accept *that flower / a flower*. Do not penalise spelling mistakes if the intention is clear.	I
6	**We like healthy food.** ✓ **Our kind teacher never shouts.** ✓	I

Pages 19–20 Joining Words		
I	and ✓	I
2	or ✓	I
3	**Jamie** <u>*and*</u> **Alfie were allowed to play outside,** <u>*but*</u> **Orla had to finish her work.**	I
4	but ✓	I
5	and, but, or ✓	I

Pages 21–22 Using *when*, *if*, *that* and *because*		
I	when ✓	I
2	because ✓	I
3	**I always clap** <u>*when / if*</u> **the team scores.** <u>*If / When*</u> **they are losing, I cheer them along.**	I I
4	that ✓	I
5	because, when ✓	I
6	**I was given a special award** <u>*because / when*</u> **I got all my spellings right.** **My teacher knew** <u>*that*</u> **I had worked really hard.**	I I

Pages 23–24 Past and Present Tense		
I	cycled were	I
2	present tense ✓	I
3	**Jake** <u>*likes*</u> **jigsaw puzzles.**	I

Answers

4	Sentence	Past tense	Present tense		I
	Charlotte tried hard to learn her spellings.	✓			
	My brother has blue eyes and blond hair.		✓		
	There are thirty children in my class.		✓		

5	Sami _threw_ the ball to Mabel.	I

6	washes dries	I

Pages 25–26 Continuous Action

I	were quacking swam	I

2	The children _were running_ across the playground. Madeleine _was brushing_ her hair.	I I

3	Matthew _was eating_ an apple when the phone rang.	I

4	_The children _are working_ hard to learn their times tables._	I

5	I told her we _were trying_ to eat more fruit. Mum said she _was feeling_ happier about our next visit to the dentist	I I

Pages 27–28 Using Tenses I

I	Our class went outside and played games. ✓	I

2	Last week, we went to the cinema and _watched / saw_ Spiderman.	I

3	Yesterday, we <u>go</u> to the library to choose some books. I <u>pick</u> an adventure story and Maddie chose a book about tigers. When we <u>get</u> home, we started to read them before we had our dinner.	I

4	Last week, we _sang_ in assembly then walked quietly back to our classroom. Allow minor copying errors as long as 'sang' is correct.	I

5	When I go on holiday, I always take a book. ✓	I

6	Answers will vary. Examples: Usually, Dad _takes / drives_ us to school. On Fridays, we _take / ride_ our bikes. (present)	I

Page 29 Using Tenses 2

I	walking ✓	I

2	As we were eating our picnic, it _started_ to rain.	I

3	Last night, the wind _blew_ wildly.	I

4	Sentence	Past tense	Present tense		I
	Uncle James was washing his car.	✓			
	Our teacher marked our work.	✓			
	We like running down the hill in the park.		✓		

Pages 30–32 Progress Test I

I	I like cereal for breakfast. ✓	I

2	were dancing were singing	I

3	Katia and I waved at <u>the girl on the bus</u>.	I

4

4	I (tidied) my bedroom last night. I (hung) my clothes in the wardrobe and (put) my toys in the basket under my bed.	1
5	adverb ✓	1
6	when ✓	1
7	_wildly_ _sadly_	1
8	There were (cows), (chickens) and (rabbits) in the same (barn).	1
9	Boris _and_ Anna like sports, _but_ Nadine prefers reading.	1
10	We _are writing_ stories about dungeons and dragons.	1
11	a command ✓	1

Pages 33–34 Punctuation Marks 1		
1	Answers will vary. Examples: _Because it is the end of the sentence. / To show it's the end of the sentence._	1
2	(We) are going to visit our grandparents at the weekend. Answers may vary. Examples: _Because it is the start of the sentence. / To show it's the start of a new sentence._	1 1
3	Finlay's Mum took him to the park. He played on the slide for a while, then he got bored. He tried the swings but they were broken. Finlay was so disappointed that Mum promised to take him swimming that night.	1
4	Our teacher, Mr Smith, read us a story about a lion.	1
5	_We had popcorn and juice at the party._ _My brother Sam won a prize._ Allow minor copying errors as long as both sentences start with a capital letter and have a full stop at the end.	1 1
6	question mark ✓	1

Pages 35–36 Punctuation Marks 2		
1	Answers will vary. Examples: _They are names. / They are names of a person and a place. / They are proper nouns._	1
2	Ciaran and Megan are going to⊙ Scotland for a holiday. They haven't been⊙ before⊙ so they are really excited.	1
3	My best friend, Rob, doesn't like ice cream. ✓	1
4	Answers will vary. Examples: _It is the name of a person. / It is someone's name. / It is a proper noun._	1
5	_There are some new books in our library._ _The teacher gave the book to Dylan._ Allow minor copying errors as long as both sentences and 'Dylan' start with capital letters and both sentences end with a full stop.	1 1
6	full stop ✓	1

Pages 37–38 Punctuation Marks 3		
1	exclamation mark ✓	1

Answers

2	*I went to York last Saturday and I visited the museum.* Allow minor copying errors as long as the capital letters and full stop are correct.	I
3	**What a fantastic surprise to see you!**	I
4	Answers will vary. Examples: *It is a name. / It is the name of a country. / It is a proper noun.*	I
5	**You're seven years old, aren't you?**	I
6	full stop ✓	I

Pages 39–40 Commas in Lists		
I	**We packed our swimming costumes, goggles and towels.**	I
2	**My book is all about ladybirds, spiders and ants. ✓**	I
3	**We need to buy flour, cherries, eggs and sugar to make the cake.**	I
4	**I like learning about animals, insects and fish. ✓**	I
5	**We brought apples, oranges and pears to the harvest festival.**	I
6	*We visited a castle, a farm, a lake and a waterpark on our trip.* Allow minor copying errors as long as the commas are correct.	I

Pages 41–42 Apostrophes to Show Belonging		
I	**to show that the jumper belongs to Sol ✓**	I
2	**Abby's new shoes are very nice. ✓**	I
3	✓ ↓ **Our dogs collar is blue with white spots.**	I
4	**The girl's hands were injured when she fell off her bike. ✓**	I
5	**We all watched Grace's dance performance.**	I
6	**The magician's wand cast two special spells.**	I

Pages 43–44 Apostrophes to Show Missing Letters		
I	**Mum wasn't feeling very well. ✓**	I
2	*did not – didn't* *they are – they're* *you have – you've*	I
3	**I *haven't* a clue where I left my homework.**	I
4	*he's* *won't* *they've*	I
5	**There's a lot of mess on the table. ✓**	I
6	**Mum said we *couldn't* play outside because it was raining.**	I

Pages 45–47 Progress Test 2		
I	*can't* *don't* *wouldn't*	I
2	**Mum chopped some potatoes, carrots, cabbage and onions.**	I
3	**We've been here before, haven't we?**	I

4	full stop ✓	I
5	Our neighbour (is mowing) the grass.	I
6	Yesterday, we visited our grandparents. They live beside the sea in a big house. I love running up and down the sand dunes and paddling in the waves. Mum said we can go again in the summer.	I
7	The young children (danced) and (sang) in the hall.	I
8	My birthday is in March and Freya's is in October. ✓	I
9	question mark ✓	I
10	Karen's eyes are blue. ✓	I
11	The boy's name is Mo.	I

	Pages 48–49 Suffixes I	
I	As we were play_ing_ in the park, it started to rain.	I
2	Yesterday, Alice jump_ed_ into the swimming pool.	I
3	Ciara is small, Guy is smaller but Sid is the small_est_.	I
4	Fred is tall but Bertie is even tall_er_.	I
5	We brought our book_s_ to the library.	I

6					I
	Adjective	**Add –er**	**Add –est**		
	happy	**happier**	**happiest**		
	funny	_funnier_	_funniest_		
	sunny	_sunnier_	_sunniest_		
	messy	_messier_	_messiest_		

7					I
	Verb	**Add –ing**	**Add –ed**		
	pat	**patting**	**patted**		
	trip	_tripping_	_tripped_		
	trim	_trimming_	_trimmed_		
	plod	_plodding_	_plodded_		

	Pages 50–51 Suffixes 2	
I	Samir was very care_ful_ / care_less_ as he coloured in his picture.	I
2	The class read quiet_ly_ while the teacher gave out the books.	I
3	The children got a lot of en_joy_ment from playing in the snow.	I
4	Tania put all the bricks back in the box_es_.	I
5	This little pig is fat but the one over there is even _fatter_.	I
6	It was a hot, _sunny_ day when we went to the seaside.	I

	Page 52 The Prefix _un–_	
I	Abby _untied_ her shoelaces.	I
2	Answers will vary. Examples: _It means Beth wasn't kind. / It means the opposite._	I

Answers

3	I was <u>un</u>happy when it rained.	I
4	Jake was <u>un</u>certain where he had left his school bag.	I
5	Answers will vary. Examples: *It means you can't stop the spell. / The spell can't be undone. / It means the opposite.*	I
Page 53 Compound Words		
I	**white – board** **play – ground** **car – park**	I
2	Seb kicked the <u>foot</u>ball into the nets.	I
3	My dad packed a <u>suit</u>case for the trip.	I
4	Answers will vary. Examples: *sunshine / sunhat / sunrise / sunbeam* *rainfall / raincoat / rainbow* *teapot / teatime / teaspoon*	I
Pages 54–56 Progress Test 3		
I	We were <u>sing</u>ing on the bus on the way home.	I
2	The <u>drummer</u> was playing the drums.	I
3	Cinderella was granted three <u>wish</u>es by the fairy godmother.	I
4	The tap <u>dripped</u> all night long.	I
5	The Queen was feeling <u>unwell</u> after she had eaten too much at the King's birthday feast.	I
6	**hope – less** **improve – ment** **tight – ly**	I
7	The brown (dog) ran happily across the (fields).	I
8	Will is tall but Sam is even <u>tall</u>er. Magda is shorter than Sofia but Kendra is the <u>short</u>est.	I
9	Answers may vary. Examples: *firework / firewood* *moonbeam / moonlight* *doorknob / doorway* *bathroom / bathtime*	I
10	*madly* *loudly* *bravely* *strangely*	I

Using Tenses 2

1 Tick the correct word to complete the sentence below.

As Will was _____ across the field, he spotted a large bull.

Tick **one.**

walked ☐

walk ☐

walking ☐

walks ☐

◯ 1 mark

2 Write the verb <u>start</u> in the **correct tense** to complete the sentence below.

As we were eating our picnic, it _____ to rain. ◯ 1 mark

3 Write the verb <u>blow</u> in the **correct tense** to complete the sentence below.

Last night, the wind _____ wildly. ◯ 1 mark

4 Tick to show whether each sentence is in the **past tense** or the **present tense**.

Sentence	Past tense	Present tense
Uncle James was washing his car.		
Our teacher marked our work.		
We like running down the hill in the park.		

◯ 1 mark

Total marks .... /4   How am I doing? ☺ 😐 😖

29

Progress Test 1

1 Tick the sentence that is a **statement**.

Tick **one**.

I like cereal for breakfast. ☐

You like porridge, don't you? ☐

Try some of mine. ☐

How tasty it is! ☐

◯ 1 mark

2 Circle the correct verbs so that the sentence is in the **past tense**.

Some performers | were dancing | | are dancing | while others

| are singing | | were singing | songs.

◯ 1 mark

3 Underline the **noun phrase** in the sentence below.

Katia and I waved at the girl on the bus.

◯ 1 mark

4 Circle the **verbs** in the passage below.

I tidied my bedroom last night. I hung my clothes in the wardrobe and put my toys in the basket under my bed.

◯ 1 mark

5 What type of word is underlined in the sentence below?

Mum was waving <u>frantically</u> to me as the bus drove off.

Tick **one.**

adverb ☐

adjective ☐

verb ☐

noun ☐

◯ I mark

6 Tick the correct word to complete the sentence below.

It was sunny _____ we arrived at the seaside.

Tick **one.**

or ☐

but ☐

because ☐

when ☐

◯ I mark

7 Add a **suffix** to each word to make an **adverb**.

Write the new word on the line.

wild _____

sad _____

◯ I mark

31

8 Circle the **nouns** in the sentence below.

There were cows, chickens and rabbits in the same barn. ◯
1 mark

9 Write one word on each line below to join the words and clauses to make a sentence.

Boris _____ Anna like sports, _____ Nadine prefers reading. ◯
1 mark

10 Write the verb <u>write</u> in the **present tense** to show a **continuous action**.

We _____ stories about dungeons and dragons. ◯
1 mark

11 What type of sentence is below? The end punctuation is covered.

Throw the ball to me now▮

Tick **one.**

an exclamation ☐

a question ☐

a command ☐

a statement ☐
◯
1 mark

Total marks .... /11   How am I doing?

32

Punctuation Marks 1

1 Why is there a **full stop** after the underlined word?

Ushma and I like dancing, swimming and playing <u>tennis</u>.

_____

_____

○ 1 mark

2 Circle the word that should start with a **capital letter** in the sentence below.

we are going to visit our grandparents at the weekend.

Why should the word you have circled start with a capital letter?

_____

_____

○ 2 marks

3 Add **full stops** in the correct places.

Finlay's Mum took him to the park He played on the slide for a while, then he got bored He tried the swings but they were broken Finlay was so disappointed that Mum promised to take him swimming that night

○ 1 mark

Punctuation Marks 1

4 Which sentence is punctuated correctly?

Tick **one.**

Our teacher, mr smith, read us a story about a lion. ☐

our teacher, mr smith, read us a story about a lion. ☐

Our teacher, Mr Smith, read us a story about a lion. ☐

Our teacher, Mr smith, read us a story about a lion ☐

◯ I mark

5 Write out each sentence and add the **correct punctuation**.

we had popcorn and juice at the party

_____

my brother sam won a prize

_____

◯ 2 marks

6 Which punctuation mark completes the sentence below?

What are you laughing at

Tick **one.**

full stop ☐

exclamation mark ☐

question mark ☐

comma ☐

◯ I mark

Total marks .... / 8   How am I doing?

Punctuation Marks 2

1 Why do the underlined words start with a **capital letter**?

Last week, <u>Ciara</u> went with her mum to <u>London</u>.

_____

_____

○ I mark

2 Circle the **full stops** that are in the wrong places.

One has been done for you.

Ciaran and Megan are going to⊙ Scotland for a holiday.

They haven't been. before. so they are really excited.

○ I mark

3 Which sentence is punctuated correctly?

Tick **one.**

my best friend, Rob, doesn't like ice cream ☐

My best friend, Rob, doesn't like ice cream. ☐

My best friend, rob, doesn't like ice cream. ☐

My Best Friend, Rob, doesn't like ice cream ☐

○ I mark

Punctuation Marks 2

4 Why does the underlined word start with a **capital letter?**

My auntie, <u>Sarah</u>, is getting married.

_____

_____ ◯
1 mark

5 Write out each sentence and add the **correct punctuation.**

there are some new books in our library

_____

the teacher gave the book to Dylan

_____ ◯
2 marks

6 Which punctuation mark completes the statement below?

Insects have six legs

Tick **one.**

full stop ☐

exclamation mark ☐

question mark ☐

comma ☐

◯
1 mark

| Total marks ..../7 | How am I doing? | | | |

Punctuation Marks 3

1 Which punctuation mark completes the sentence below?

How well you look

Tick **one.**

full stop ☐

exclamation mark ☐

question mark ☐

comma ☐

○
1 mark

2 Rewrite this sentence using the correct punctuation.

i went to York last saturday and i visited the museum

_____

_____

○
1 mark

3 Write the missing punctuation mark to complete the sentence below.

What a fantastic surprise to see you

○
1 mark

Punctuation Marks 3

4 Why does the underlined word start with a **capital letter?**

In the summer, we are going to <u>France</u> for two weeks.

_____

_____ ◯
                                                  1 mark

5 Write the missing punctuation mark to complete the sentence below.

You're seven years old, aren't you   ◯
                                                            1 mark

6 Which punctuation mark completes the sentence below?

Take your muddy shoes off before you come inside

Tick **one.**

full stop   ▢

apostrophe   ▢

question mark   ▢

comma   ▢   ◯
                                                          1 mark

Total marks .... /6   How am I doing?

Commas in Lists

1 Add one **comma** to the sentence below in the correct place.

We packed our swimming costumes goggles and towels. ◯
1 mark

2 Which sentence is punctuated correctly?

Tick **one**.

My book is all about ladybirds, spiders and ants. ☐

My book, is all about ladybirds, spiders and ants. ☐

My book is all about ladybirds, spiders and, ants. ☐

My book, is all about, ladybirds, spiders, and ants. ☐ ◯
1 mark

3 Add **commas** to the sentence below in the correct places.

We need to buy flour cherries eggs and sugar to make the cake. ◯
1 mark

Commas in Lists

4 Which sentence is punctuated correctly?

Tick **one.**

I like learning about animals, insects and fish.

I like, learning about, animals, insects and fish.

I like, learning about animals, insects and fish.

I like learning, about animals, insects and fish.

 I mark

5 Add **one comma** to the sentence below in the correct place.

We brought apples oranges and pears to the harvest festival.

 I mark

6 The **commas** are in the wrong place in the sentence below.

Rewrite the sentence, putting the **commas** in the correct places.

We visited, a castle, a farm a lake, and a waterpark on our trip.

_____

_____

I mark

Total marks .... /6   How am I doing?

40

Apostrophes to Show Belonging

1 Why has an **apostrophe** been used in the sentence below?

Sol's jumper was dirty.

Tick **one.**

to show that Sol belongs to the jumper ☐

to show that the jumper belongs to Sol ☐

because Sol's means Sol is ☐

because Sol is someone's name ☐

1 mark

2 Which sentence uses an **apostrophe** correctly?

Tick **one.**

Abby's new shoes are very nice. ☐

Abbys' new shoes are very nice. ☐

Abbys new shoe's are very nice. ☐

Abbys new shoes' are very nice. ☐

1 mark

3 Tick one box to show where an **apostrophe** should go in the sentence below.

☐ ☐   ☐

Our dogs collar is blue with white spots.

1 mark

41

Apostrophes to Show Belonging

4 Which sentence uses an **apostrophe** correctly?

Tick **one.**

The girls hands' were injured when she fell off her bike. ☐

The girls hand's were injured when she fell off her bike. ☐

The girls' hands were injured when she fell off her bike. ☐

The girl's hands were injured when she fell off her bike. ☐ ◯
1 mark

5 Add one **apostrophe** to the sentence below in the correct place.

We all watched Graces dance performance. ◯
1 mark

6 Add one **apostrophe** to the sentence below in the correct place.

The magicians wand cast two special spells. ◯
1 mark

Total marks .... /6   How am I doing?

Apostrophes to Show Missing Letters

1 Which sentence uses an **apostrophe** correctly?

Tick **one.**

Mum was'nt feeling very well. ☐

Mum wasn't feeling very well. ☐

Mum wasnt' feeling very well. ☐

Mum wasnt feeling very we'll. ☐

○ 1 mark

2 Draw lines to match the groups of words that have the same meaning.

One has been done for you.

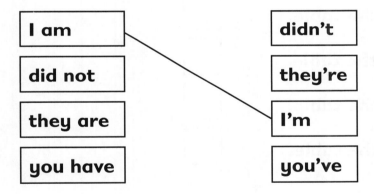

○ 1 mark

3 Write the words <u>have not</u> as one word, using an **apostrophe**.

I _____ a clue where I left my homework.

○ 1 mark

43

Apostrophes to Show Missing Letters

4 Write each pair of words as one word, using an **apostrophe**.

One has been done for you.

we had	<u>we'd</u>
he is	
will not	
they have	

5 Which sentence uses an **apostrophe** correctly?

Tick **one.**

There's a lot of mess on the table. ☐

Theres' a lot of mess on the table. ☐

Ther'es a lot of mess on the table. ☐

Theres a lot of mes's on the table. ☐

I mark

6 Write the words <u>could not</u> as one word, using an **apostrophe**.

Mum said we _____ play outside because it was raining. I mark

1 Write each pair of words as one word, using an **apostrophe**.

can not	
do not	
would not	

I mark

2 Add **commas** to the sentence below in the correct places.

Mum chopped some potatoes carrots cabbage and onions.

I mark

3 Write the missing punctuation mark to complete the sentence below.

We've been here before, haven't we

I mark

4 Which punctuation mark completes the sentence below?

Bring me your homework, please

Tick **one.**

full stop ☐

apostrophe ☐

question mark ☐

comma ☐

I mark

5 Circle the correct verbs so that the sentence is in the **present tense**.

Our neighbour | **was mowing** | | **is mowing** | **the grass.**

I mark

6 Add **full stops** in the correct places.

Yesterday, we visited our grandparents They live beside the sea in a big house I love running up and down the sand dunes and paddling in the waves Mum said we can go again in the summer

○ I mark

7 Circle the **verbs** in the sentence below.

The young children danced and sang in the hall.

○ I mark

8 Which sentence is punctuated correctly?

Tick **one.**

My birthday is in march and Freya's is in october. ☐

My birthday is in March and freya's is in October. ☐

My birthday is in March and Freya's is in October. ☐

My Birthday is in march and Freya's is in october. ☐

○ I mark

9 Which punctuation mark completes the statement below?

We are going to the cinema tonight, aren't we

Tick **one.**

full stop ☐

exclamation mark ☐

question mark ☐

comma ☐

◯ I mark

10 Which sentence uses an **apostrophe** correctly?

Tick **one.**

Karen's eyes are blue. ☐

Karens' eyes are blue. ☐

Karens eye's are blue. ☐

Karens eyes' are blue. ☐

◯ I mark

11 Add one **apostrophe** to the sentence below in the correct place.

The   boys   name   is   Mo.

◯ I mark

Total marks .... /11   How am I doing?   ☺ 😐 😣

Suffixes 1

1 Add a **suffix** to the word <u>play</u> to complete the sentence below.

As we were <u>play</u>_____ in the park, it started to rain.

◯ 1 mark

2 Add a **suffix** to the word <u>jump</u> to complete the sentence below.

Yesterday, Alice <u>jump</u>_____ into the swimming pool.

◯ 1 mark

3 Add a **suffix** to the word <u>small</u> to complete the sentence below.

Ciara is small, Guy is smaller but Sid is the <u>small</u>_____.

◯ 1 mark

4 Add a **suffix** to the word <u>tall</u> to complete the sentence below.

Fred is tall but Bertie is even <u>tall</u>_____.

◯ 1 mark

5 Add **s** or **es** to make the word <u>book</u> a plural.

We brought our <u>book</u>_____ to the library.

◯ 1 mark

Suffixes 1

6 Complete the table by adding the **suffixes –est** and **–er** to each adjective.

One has been done for you.

Adjective	Add –er	Add –est
happy	<u>happier</u>	<u>happiest</u>
funny		
sunny		
messy		

1 mark

7 Complete the table by adding the **suffixes –ing** and **–ed** to each verb.

One has been done for you.

Verb	Add –ing	Add –ed
pat	<u>patting</u>	<u>patted</u>
trip		
trim		
plod		

1 mark

Total marks .... /7   How am I doing?

49

Suffixes 2

1 Add a **suffix** to the word <u>care</u> to complete the sentence below.

Samir was very <u>care</u>＿＿＿＿＿ as he coloured in his picture. ◯ I mark

2 Add a **suffix** to the adjective <u>quiet</u> to make an adverb and complete the sentence below.

The class read <u>quiet</u>＿＿＿＿＿ while the teacher gave out the books. ◯ I mark

3 Add a **suffix** to the word <u>enjoy</u> to complete the sentence below.

The children got a lot of <u>enjoy</u>＿＿＿＿＿ from playing in the snow. ◯ I mark

4 Add a **suffix** to make the word <u>box</u> a plural.

Tania put all the bricks back in the <u>box</u>＿＿＿＿＿. ◯ I mark

5 Write the word <u>fat</u> with a **suffix** to complete the sentence below.
Remember to change the spelling if needed.

This little pig is fat but the one over there is even ＿＿＿＿＿. ◯ I mark

6 Write the word <u>sun</u> with a **suffix** to complete the sentence below.
Remember to change the spelling if needed.

It was a hot, ＿＿＿＿＿ day when we went to the seaside. ◯ I mark

Total marks .... /6   How am I doing? ☺ 😐 ☹

The Prefix un-

1 Add a **prefix** to the word <u>tied</u> to show that Abby was taking her shoes off.

Abby _____<u>tied</u> **her shoelaces.**

○ I mark

2 How does the **prefix** <u>un</u> change the meaning of the word <u>kind</u> in the sentence below?

Beth was <u>unkind</u> to her brother.

_____

_____ ○ I mark

3 Add a **prefix** to the word <u>happy</u> to make a word with the opposite meaning.

I was _____<u>happy</u> **when it rained.**

○ I mark

4 Add a **prefix** to the word <u>certain</u> to show that Jake wasn't sure where he had left his school bag.

Jake was _____<u>certain</u> **where he had left his school bag.**

○ I mark

5 How does the prefix <u>un</u> change the meaning of the word <u>do</u> in the sentence below?

Once the spell has been cast, it is impossible to <u>undo</u>.

_____

_____ ○ I mark

Total marks .... /5   How am I doing? ☺ 😐 😣

51

Compound Words

1 Draw lines to match pairs of words that make **compound words**.

One has been done for you.

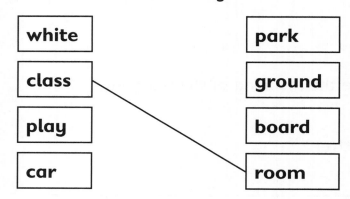

white		park
class		ground
play		board
car		room

 I mark

2 Add a **word** to <u>foot</u> to make a **compound word** and complete the sentence below.

Seb kicked the <u>foot</u>_____ into the nets.

 I mark

3 Add a **word** to <u>suit</u> to make a **compound word** and complete the sentence below.

My dad packed a <u>suit</u>_____ for the trip.

 I mark

4 Add a **word** to each noun to make a **compound word**.

One has been done for you.

Noun	Compound word
black	<u>blackberry</u>
sun	
rain	
tea	

 I mark

Total marks .... /4   How am I doing?

52

1 Add a **suffix** to the word <u>sing</u> to complete the sentence below.

We were <u>sing</u>_____ on the bus on the way home.

◯ I mark

2 Write the word <u>drum</u> with a **suffix** to complete the sentence below.

Remember to change the spelling if needed.

The _____ was playing the drums.

◯ I mark

3 Write **s** or **es** to make the word <u>wish</u> a plural.

Cinderella was granted three <u>wish</u>_____ by the fairy godmother.

◯ I mark

4 Write the word <u>drip</u> with a **suffix** to complete the sentence below in the **past tense**.

Remember to change the spelling if needed.

The tap _____ all night long.

◯ I mark

5 Add a **prefix** to the word <u>well</u> to show that the Queen was not feeling very well.

The Queen was feeling _____ after she had eaten too much at the King's birthday feast.

1 mark

6 Draw a line to match each word to the correct **suffix**.

One has been done for you.

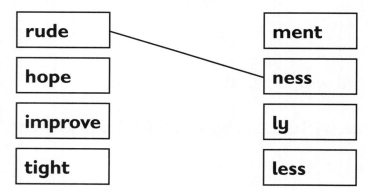

rude	ment
hope	ness
improve	ly
tight	less

1 mark

7 Circle the **nouns** in the sentence below.

The brown dog ran happily across the fields.

1 mark

8 Add a different **suffix** to each underlined word to complete the sentences below.

Will is tall but Sam is even <u>tall</u>_____.

Magda is shorter than Sofia but Kendra is the <u>short</u>_____.

1 mark

9 Add a **word** to each noun to make a **compound word**.

Write the new words on the right in the table.

Noun	Compound word
fire	
moon	
door	
bath	

1 mark

10 Add a **suffix** to each adjective to make an **adverb**.

Write the new words on the right in the table.

Adjective	Adverb
mad	
loud	
brave	
strange	

1 mark

Total marks .... /10   How am I doing?

Progress Test Charts

Progress Test 1

Q	Topic	✔ or ✗	See Pages
1	Sentence Types		9–14
2	Past and Present Tense		23–24
3	Noun Phrases		17–18
4	Word Classes		4–8
5	Word Classes		4–8
6	Using *when*, *if*, *that* and *because*		21–22
7	Word Classes		4–8
8	Word Classes		4–8
9	Joining Words		19–20
10	Continuous Action		25–26
11	Sentence Types		9–14

Progress Test 3

Q	Topic	✔ or ✗	See Pages
1	Suffixes		48–50
2	Suffixes		48–50
3	Suffixes		48–50
4	Suffixes; Past and Present Tense		48–50; 23–24
5	The Prefix *un–*		51
6	Suffixes		48–50
7	Word Classes		4–8
8	Suffixes		48–50
9	Compound Words		52
10	Suffixes		48–50

Progress Test 2

Q	Topic	✔ or ✗	See Pages
1	Apostrophes to Show Missing Letters		43–44
2	Punctuation Marks		33–38
3	Punctuation Marks		33–38
4	Punctuation Marks		33–38
5	Past and Present Tense		23–24
6	Punctuation Marks		33–38
7	Word Classes		4–8
8	Punctuation Marks		33–38
9	Punctuation Marks		33–38
10	Apostrophes to Show Belonging		41–42
11	Apostrophes to Show Belonging		41–42

What am I doing well in?

_____

_____

_____

What do I need to improve?

_____

_____

_____

56